OVERCOMING

DEPRESSION:

Depressed Not Defeated.

KING M. KENNEDY

DEDICATION

This book is dedicated to God who gave me the grace and strength to pull through the difficult moments of my life

To everyone who is fighting against depression I believe in you and I know that you are a champion as long as you keep pushing

TABLE OF CONTENTS

Title Page
Copyright
Dedication
Contents

INTRODUCTION

★ Have you ever tried overcoming your depression? Or are you about to give up because it failed? Do you worry others are pulling through but you can not figure how to?

Well I also thought it is impossible but here I am feeling good despite all I have been through and I am sure you also want to experience that feeling of happiness too

So in this book you are holding right now I am going to be discussing the causes the symptoms for those who are yet to realise that they are no longer grieving but already depressed there is a thin line between depression and grieving) and give simple solutions that will help you find your way out the dark tunnel called depression

Sometimes you think it is no longer there but boom There you have it weighing you down and you realise those moments were just an illusion I have also been through those times and I can relate how painful it feels when you realise that it is just a facade Right now I am going to hold your hands through this book and lead you to that land of freedom where you will experience peace and joy all around every day

So if you like you can get a pen and notebook to write down the key points which I am going to be giving you It is more preferable to memorizing them and you can easily relate them to your situation as it feels

CHAPTER ONE

DEPRESSION

Depression is a health condition that affects the mental and physical health for more than two weeks You can also call it a widespread mental health disorder When you have that persistent feeling of sadness guilt worthlessness or hopelessness you are feeling depressed already without even realizing it

Many people disregard it and may feel that it is just a grieving period that will pass while some are afraid to accept that they are depressed because they think that death is the next thing coming But that view is wrong You can be depressed for months or years without committing suicide Although you may have suicidal thoughts or feelings that no one cares about you

While I was depressed I often thought nobody loved me and I would stay away from others thinking I would feel better But have you ever thought that isolating oneself is like feeding those flames of depression ignited in you? Just like you I thought self isolation was the best way to cope with it

> ★ As we move on in this book I will be giving certain things you have to do and of course what to avoid in overcoming depression

CHAPTER TWO

CAUSES OF DEPRESSION

There are so many reasons why people become depressed but we will take the basic and common ones that we are familiar with to avoid going too deep Our goal is not only identifying the causes but also the symptoms while we take the solutions which is our greatest goal; overcoming depression

The first cause of depression I am going to talk about is:

GRIEF >

Well many of us are familiar with this and will probably have experienced it one time or another Grief varies; it can be on the surface intense short or prolonged Often times it is the intense and prolonged griefs that leads to depression And at times grief can just be a means to setback when overcoming depression

When I was trying to overcome depression I lost someone very dear to me and that was how I relapsed I fell back to the ground level and almost gave up By then it became more worse and difficult trying to get over it

- ❖ Grief can come as a result of:
- ➢ The loss of a loved one
- ➢ The loss of a relationship

➤ The loss of financial status job or societal status Yeah falling from grace to grass or failure to maintain a particular status quo can lead to intense grief which may give room for depression When the breadwinner of a family loses his source of income and the family can hardly get by the person may become depressed and even pick up certain habits like drinking or smoking in order to cope

CHAPTER THREE
LOW SELF-ESTEEM

Right now you may be thinking that low self -esteem is just a symptom of depression Yeah but it also can lead to severe depression if not well addressed When I was depressed I also thought that my low self-esteem was caused by depression Later I realised that due to criticisms and guilts of not being good enough I had a very low self-esteem and self worth and that often triggered my depression

❖ There are different causes of low self-esteem

> Criticisms: Although there are good and constructive criticisms the negative and unchecked ones do more harm than good to a person's self worth When you are often criticised or faulted especially by a particular person you start to lose confidence in yourself Self doubts creep in and as time goes on you begin to lose your value and feel unsatisfied with yourself Even before you are accused you already blame yourself
Sounds depressing right? Negative criticisms never encourages you to do better Rather they affect your performance in the opposite direction
> Feeling Weird or Left Out Circumstances beyond our control like family background financial status gender and individual differences often create a division among peers I remember how I felt when many of my friends were talking about vacations and outings but I couldn't contribute because I am a stay-at-home person

It often happens and most times we can't help it Sometimes when your ideology or opinion about certain things contrast with others you feel left out or side tracked and if the other party aren't accepting or mature enough you might be left behind or excluded Unfortunately we all can't be wise or open-minded enough to accept that other people's views can differ and shouldn't impose ours on them If this goes on for a long timme without someone to give you assurance that you are not abnormal it can lead to depression

I believe that is clear enough to dispel any doubts or confusion about how low self-esteem can lead to depression So let us proceed to the next cause of depression

CHAPTER FOUR

PAST OR REPETITIVE FAILURES

Inability to succeed at a particular thing or failure at different occasions can lead to lack of self worth and trigger depression Some people may say that you are being jinxed or unlucky but they forget that life is neither fair nor unfair to anybody Sometimes unfavourable situations keep happening or when you do not get desired results from something you start to feel like there is something wrong with you Inability to accept failure and start over again can lead to depression

* Also our behaviour and temperament plays an important role in coping with failure

We have four major temperaments although you can end up with traits from each one But basically we have the Sanguine the Choleric Melancholic and the Phlegmatic

- ❖ The Melancholics are the most easily depressed among them all They are the <u>SUBMISSIVE UNFRIENDLY</u> that is they only give in harshly and often keep to themselves They are pessimistic and have an unfair view of life especially when things are not going smoothly

★

★ Understanding your temperament will help you to know how easily depressed you can get and practical exercises you can do to overcome it Although you will need to read extensively on books about Temperaments and Behaviours because the subject is a large one Book like "WHY YOU ACT THE WAY YOU DO by Tim LaHaye " gives you a clear insight into what makes up your temperament and helps you in discovering the real you not a biased view from others But never fear I am going to give you solutions to overcoming depression regardless of your temperament You will also need practical exercises to engage in to becoming a depression free person

❖ Sanguines are hardly depressed and often feel great because they live a carefree life and are open-minded like they literally "roll with the punches" They are always full of life and vigour But they can also fall into depression and can be easily discovered

- ❖ Cholerics can be depressed easily because they always have this notion that everything they do must be perfect If things do not go the way they want or expect depression can set in
- ❖ Phlegmatics are open-minded and can often go with the way life leads They also keep to themselves but can be the perfect friend for any of the other temperament This is because they are <u>SUBMISSIVE FRIENDLY</u>
- ★ Sanguines are <u>DOMINANT FRIENDLY</u> while Cholerics are <u>DOMINANT UNFRIENDLY</u>

CHAPTER FIVE

SYMPTOMS OF DEPRESSION

Identifying the symptoms of your depression is very essential to overcoming it Before any prescription can be given for any illness the symptoms must be known to avoid wrong prescription Accepting that you are depressed no matter how hard it feels and recognizing the signs is a crucial step to freedom

This is because you will need to change certain habits that you do when your depression is triggered

➢ Self Isolation Wanting to be alone every time because you are feeling down is one of the key symptoms of depression When you are deliberately distancing yourself from others or avoiding gatherings or peers you are already trailing the lane of depression Absenting yourself from the midst of people you love or occasions you always yearned for is one thing to look for if you suspect that you are depressed

- Lack of Interest In Hobbies Or Things You Enjoy. Before I became overwhelmed with depression I prayed everyday and loved singing Later I stopped praying and stayed away from music for a long time It took me some time before I discovered that I had become a shadow of myself The moment you start avoiding the gym although you love working out stopped baking reading or doing things you normally engage in; you are getting neck deep in depression and you need to seek professional help immediately
- No Concentration Lack of focus or clear mind when in school at work or among others shows that you are feeling depressed Rest assured no one is blaming you Remember you need to tick off these points to know how deep you have sank into depression

- Change In Sleeping Patterns: You may start sleeping during the day and spending all night staring into space or reminiscing about the past or other things
- Lack Of Appetite Or Eating More Than Usual: This can lead to weight loss or obesity Depression can steal your desire to eat even your favourite foods and it can make you pick up bad habits like eating into the midnight or feeding on junks You may end up being underweight or overweight So watch out for this signs
- Anxiety: Feeling anxious over nothing is a symptom of depression You may start feeling or thinking that your relationship will not last or your partner will cheat on you etc This is being insecure

- Suicidal Thoughts: This is the most dangerous symptom of depression Being depressed opens up your mind to different evil thoughts You may feel worthless useless and think you do not deserve to live or be happy Well let me tell you a secret too YOU DO NOT DESERVE TO BE SAD IN LIFE This is because You are You and nobody can take your place You need to avoid those thoughts and silence them when they come Also Daily Declarations help too Dying will only leave a void which nobody else can fill
- Up in the next chapter are things which depressed people do in order to help themselves but only end up doing more harm

CHAPTER SIX

WHAT IS NOT THE SOLUTION?

As eager and excited as I am to give the key to freedom from Depression this chapter can not be overlooked Yeah I really want to spill the beans right away I need to tell you the things that might look like the solution but they are never it and can only give temporary relief Sometimes they are harmful to our mental and physical health and others have side effects

➢ Giving Into Peer Pressure: We have already explained how others' point of view individual differences can lead to depression Now giving in to them or putting aside your beliefs or ideas on certain subjects just to be accepted is NOT a way of preventing depression When you give in you lose your value and self worth It will take a long time before you realise that your self worth is gone Also you are unique your opinion may often clash with theirs and at the end you will have to leave their circle

So why not face them up front and retain who you are? I bet you will feel refreshed

- Taking Drugs Or Alcohol: Drugs and drinks are the very worst thing to turn to when you are depressed They only give you a short-lived illusion of happiness and freedom while you are still high on them The moment your eyes are cleared the mirage is broken Instead they sink you deeper into depression If you do not stop taking them you become addicts That is like jumping from the frying pan into the fire that is making a bad situation more worse

- Resignation: This is one of the most damaging thing to do when depressed You do not handle depression my letting things be For a while before I found my out of depression I believed that accepting my date and living each day as it comes was the safe way out

But that is not living I was just existing and could hardly maintain my relationship with others Do not be deceived not taking any action leads to severe depression and makes it more difficult to overcome Tiny steps go a long way daily so even if it is baby steps Take Them Each Day They are necessary

- Withdrawal Or Socializing: Being depressed often makes you self isolate yourself which does more harm than good It gives room to evil or harmful thoughts like hurting yourself or committing suicide

  Although some people still manage to relate with others or even party every now and then it doesn't help when you stretch it It is painful how people party from dusk to dawn yet they still drown in depression It makes people think that you are okay and does not need help or attention which you really do You can socialize but do not use it as a camouflage to hide your depression

➢ Suicide: The most common action depressed people do which makes it too late for loved ones to help Trust me when I say it is not easy to resist this temptation completely You think that death relieves you of the suffering pain and hurt you are going through then If only the victims know how much they lose and people who really loved them feels they would have had a rethink I am not blaming them because I have had those thoughts countless times especially when I lost someone I really loved Life became meaningless and I thought that I had no reason to continue living Just as I was about to give up on life completely I thought of how disappointed the person would be feeling and how much hurt and pain I would cause for my family and friends Right there and then I resolved to hold on and give all it to make myself a person who they will be proud of or better still make myself proud of who I become

* Note that giving up is never the answer to depression Your existence is NOT a mistake or an accident
* There are others going through more worse situations than you are right now Also some of them were able to pull through so why can't you?
* Hold on and keep pushing till you can look back and say "I Finally Made It"; that feeling can not be compared to anything else

CHAPTER SEVEN
STEPS TO FREEDOM

You are reading this chapter means you are just a step away from your freedom Since you are ready to leave the dark out the f depression Congratulations are in order and I am sincerely happy for you Depression is not something pleasant to the human nature and it takes a lot of determination and courage to emerge victorious

You have made it this far not to give up I believe

I call them steps because you will not carry them out all at once They need to be done one after the other Also consistency is key when handling depression As minute as these baby steps may seem you need to do them repeatedly bro get the results you desire

I want you to make up your mind not to stop halfway just because you are feeling better or give up when you are not done because the improvement is not as fast as you expected But be sure that you will definitely get what you are looking for at the end

> ➢ Open Up To Your Partner Family Or Friends: There is a saying that "A problem shared is half solved" Letting your family and loved ones know what you are going through is the first step to take This is because you will be needing their love care attention support and encouragement all the way through Knowing that you are truly loved and important lifts a kind of barrier between you and also makes you feel less encumbered You become more confident that no matter what happens they have got you covered

So as difficult as that might be you need to open up to someone who you trust and feel comfortable with They will also share your thoughts and can help when you need it Having someone who understands you makes your recovery easier and less overwhelming

> Letting Them Know What You Need Telling your closed ones what you need like time to yourself when you are feeling crowded or their attention when you are lonely and other things is also crucial These are your desires we are talking about and they can not know what you want unless you speak up When you need someone to confide in look for someone you trust " Man can not live in isolation" Try to share your thoughts instead of bottling them within yourself Keeping your feelings bottled up is disastrous when depressed it can destroy the the victim By sharing your feelings you are getting closer to your goal

- Create Time To Be Together. No matter how busy you are find time to communicate with your partner or loved ones I do not mean communication as in speech alone Let them know how you are feeling the reasons why you feel that way; and also how you are coping either fine or not

Never imagine that they do not care or will not understand They love you and that is what matters Rub minds with them if you feel like or unburden your mind if you so desire Freeing your mind of the turbulent thoughts going through it is essential to having a healthy mind When you do this you feel light and free But do not stop there

➢ Avoid Relying On Substances Or Medications: This is part of what we discussed in the last chapter Taking drugs and other substances that are not prescribed by your medical practitioner can only give temporary relief and if not controlled the body may become addicted to them or develop resistance against them That is why even prescribed medications have limits Increasing the dosage in order to feel instant relief will only lead to a lifetime of taking drugs and you will become addicted to them
So unless it is carefully recommended by your doctor please avoid them

➢ Saying "No" When Not Feeling Good: You may think "but that is Self Isolation" No learning to say no to certain occasions or activities that you feel it is not constructive enough in any way is actually okay

What I mean by constructive is they do not add value to you or only put out negative vibes Parties like all-nighters that only make you feel spent with it getting better can be avoided Trying to socialize during recovery does not mean you should go out of your way to be accepted by others

Your mental physical and emotional health are what you should prioritize during this period It is not over until it is over

➢ Relaxation And Reflection: Always have time to rest daily and reflect on how far you have progressed what you need to do and exercises you can engage in to improve your moods During this period clear your mind of any harmful or work-related thoughts Just think about things you do that make you feel good and what else you love doing that can help improve your mental state

If your depression was caused by overweight why not go to the gym or take morning runs? It can be anytime as long as it is convenient for you Also exercising with friends or partner will help you get rid of that extra weight and makes it fun

If it the death of a loved one you can get a journal and start penning down your thoughts and feelings about it Talking to someone you trust will also go a long way in helping you feel better especially if the confidant is a mutual friend who also once knew the deceased

➢ Respond To Positive Invitations: Family functions a walk in the park or work outings where you feel stress-free improves your mood and can help you take your mind off your loss or grief Staying amidst people who love and care about you improves your view of life It encourages you to become a better person and stabilize you psychologically
While I was going through my depressed state I always felt better and optimistic that I could overcome my challenges whenever I was among my family and friends So birthday parties picnics family gatherings and other celebrations you should not avoid them because you NEED them

> Interaction With Your Loved Ones:
Always give room for interaction Let them know why you do what you do By sharing your reasons with them they will understand you better and view things from your perspective Do not just assume they already know or think that they will not understand Give your explanations first and see how they react Also let them contribute their thoughts on matters you are yet to decide on You never can tell their ideas may appeal to you more than the ones you have "No man is an island if knowledge" no one is perfect But if their suggestions do not sound good enough to you feel free to tell them so in a good way Do not make them feel bad or useless just explain why you can not take their suggestions and everyone will feel appreciated

Gradually we are moving towards the end of our baby but powerful steps which will bring great results

- ➢ Know When You Need Help And Seek It: You seeking for help from medical practitioners like psychologists psychotherapists and others is not a sign of weakness nor something you should be ashamed of We all need help and that is exactly why they study do research and read widely for It does not mean that you are damaged or helpless Remember you need all the help you can get because you deserve to be happy You matter do not let anyone convince you otherwise You need their assistance and they are also ready to help you whichever way you need it

The important thing to do is look for the one that you feel okay and comfortable communicating with Do not stop looking till you find the right one Do not keep things away from them You can not make much progress whan you do not feel at ease or relaxed with your therapist You need to trust them before you can confide in them

I believe you can do it You can get out of that dark tunnel and feel amazing like I also did

Actually a self-help journal will help you along the way It makes it easier to describe your feelings and lighten your mind each day Also you get to track your progress and input any other ideas you think will help

So now that we have gone through the basics of depression and finding our way out of it you can seek more help and read more about it because it is a rather broad topic Also there are different types of depression which include technical terms which you will need medical help to explain Do not be afraid to learn more about it knowing your enemy better gives you an edge over it Yes depression is an enemy we should get rid of in our society Thank you for making the effort it really counts

ABOUT THE AUTHOR

King M Kennedy is young lady and spends almost all her leisure time reading novels Although this is not her first book the need to help others live a good life is what drove her in publishing this book Overcoming depression is not an easy feat and we all need every help and encouragement in doing so

She will love to hear back from you so your reviews are very important in helping others to also take this chance to freedom Also ideas and suggestions will be welcome

Remember You Matter Everyone does in a special way

9 798369 751756